D1408082

Exciting Origami

Origami Birds

EMANUELE AZZITÀ

Enslow Publishing

101 W. 23rd Street
Suite 240
New York, NY 10011
USA

enslow.com

This edition published in 2018 by Enslow Publishing, LLC.
101 W. 23rd Street, Suite 240, New York, NY 10011

Library of Congress Cataloging-in-Publication Data
Names: Azzitá, Emanuele.
Title: Origami birds / Emanuele Azzitá
Description: New York : Enslow Publishing, 2018 | Series: Exciting origami | Includes index and bibliographical reference. | Audience: Grades 3-6.
Identifiers: ISBN 9780766086487 (library bound) | ISBN 9780766087590 (pbk.) | ISBN 9780766087606 (6 pack)
Subjects: LCSH: Origami--Juvenile literature. | Birds in art--Juvenile literature.
Classification: LCC TT872.5 A99 2018 | DDC 736/.982—dc23

Printed in the United States of America

To Our Readers: We have done our best to make sure all websites in this book were active and appropriate when we went to press. However, the author and the publisher have no control over and assume no liability for the material available on those websites or on any websites they may link to. Any comments or suggestions can be sent by e-mail to customerservice@enslow.com.

CONTENTS

INTRODUCTION 4-5

AMAZING BIRDS

- OWL 6-7
- HEN 8-11
- STORK 12-15
- PEACOCK 16-17
- CROW 18-20
- SWAN 21-23
- SWALLOW 24-29
- CRANE 30-33
- TURKEY 34-37
- SPARROW 38-39
- WILD DUCK 40-43
- PENGUIN 44-45

GLOSSARY 46

FURTHER READING 47

INDEX 48

INTRODUCTION

Origami is, simply put, the art of creating figures (people, animals, flowers, and more) using just a piece of paper. Fantasy and creativity are the key elements in origami design: prove your skills and enjoy the process of making your favorite objects out of paper—or invent your own! Get ready to create many feathered wonders, including a lovely sparrow, a charming penguin, and a darling owl. Origami is an easy hobby that requires your imagination and patience; you craft with your hands, so at first you'll need some practice. You might not achieve what you want the first time, but don't give up. After a little time, once you get the hang of it, you'll have tons of fun mastering this figure-making art. One thing's for sure—you'll spend some unforgettable afternoons making your flying friends. And while you make them you'll also experience the unique feeling of being an artist: with only your skills, a piece of paper, and a few folds, you'll create some real masterpieces. So what are you waiting for? Carefully follow the instructions and get ready to be surprised by the results. Let your fantasies soar!

MATERIAL

Origami is a great hobby you can practice anytime and with only a few materials: you just need a sheet of paper, a book, and someplace to work. Of course, you should pay attention to the quality of the paper. To make beautiful, long-lasting objects, use paper appropriate for your goal. We recommend sheets of paper that:

- *Are not too rigid, since you'll have a hard time folding them.*
- *Are not too thin, since they will tear easily.*
- *Are resistant and somewhat rigid, so you can create easy crease patterns.*

You can find high-quality paper specifically designed for origami, but you don't need this paper when you're just beginning. At first, try using:

- *Magazine paper. The pages will be full of colorful photos, adding an original and elegant touch to your creations.*
- *Construction paper.*
- *Metallic foil paper. This paper will give you an easy way to outline the edges of your figures.*
- *Wrapping paper.*

To make your creations, you need to fold the sheets carefully. If you need to, feel free to use your nails to go over each crease. This will make it easier to create lasting, defined folds. Even though scissors aren't used in traditional origami, they might be useful for some figures. Go ahead and use them if you want—don't worry about it!

OWL

1 Place a sheet of paper on a flat surface. Fold and unfold along diagonal line AC. Bring edges AB and AD toward line AC.

2 Fold the A tip inward just a little bit. Fold the B and D corners inward along lines 1 and 2.

3 Fold point C forward along the horizontal axis.

4 Now let's make the ears. Fold corners E and F backward along the dotted line. Now fold along the lines.

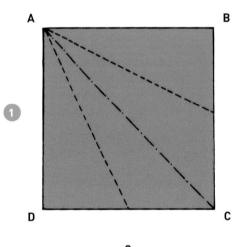

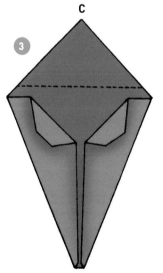

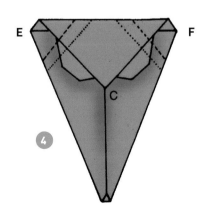

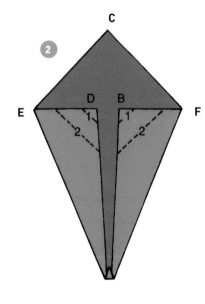

5 To make the beak, you need to fold corner C backward and then forward. Fold the uppermost line backward along the dotted line. To make the head, fold the part below the beak forward and backward.

6 Fold G and H backward. Fold tip A backward. Fold the tip forward; now you have the tail.

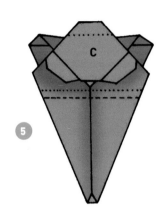

7 To make the legs, fold corners I and J backward and forward. Fold corners F and E toward the ears along the line.

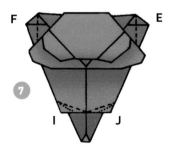

hEn

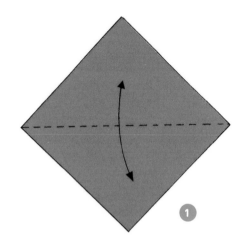

1   Fold along the lines and unfold.

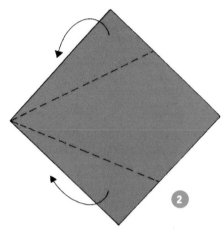

2   Fold backward.

3-4   Fold along the line.

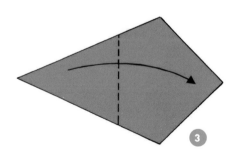

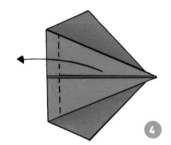

5 Fold backward along the line.

6 Fold in both directions along the line and push the tip inward.

7-10 Fold in both directions along the line, shape it, and push inward.

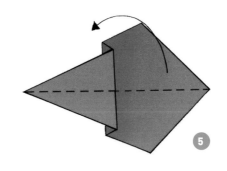

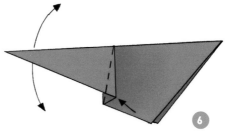

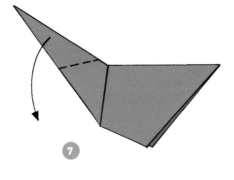

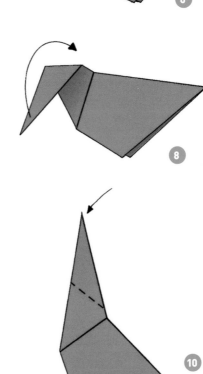

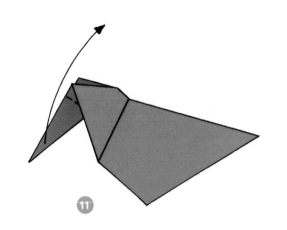

11-12 Repeat the same procedure to make the beak.

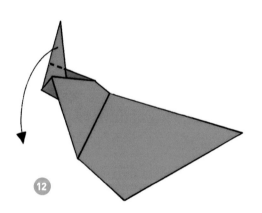

13 Lift the beak a little.

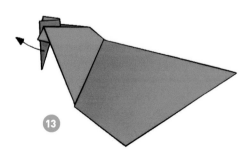

14   Fold outward.

15   Fold in both directions
along the lines and push
the tail inward.

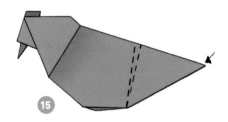

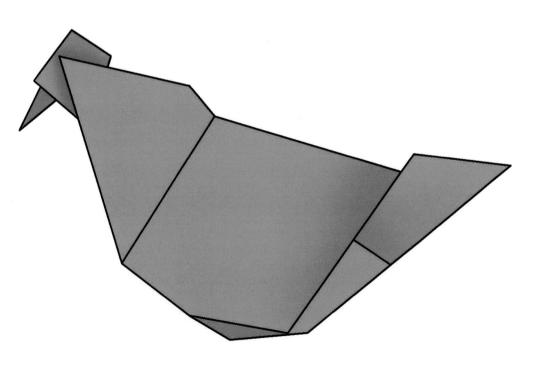

STORK

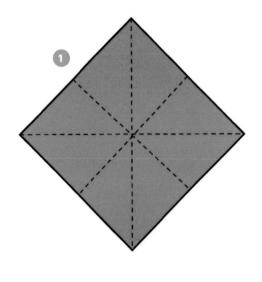

1-3 Fold square sheet along the lines.

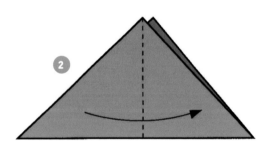

4 Lift the tip and spread out the inner part of the flap to make a square.

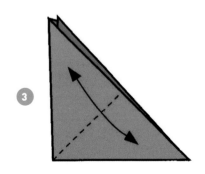

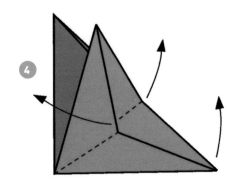

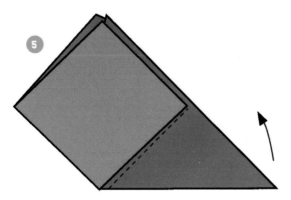

5 Repeat the same step on the other side.

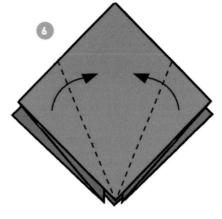

6 Fold along the lines.

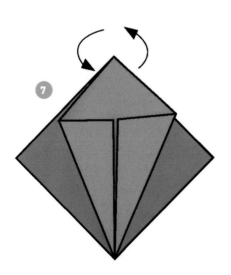

7 Flip the paper to the other side.

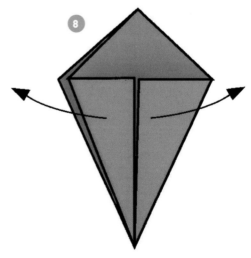

8 Repeat the last step and open the flaps.

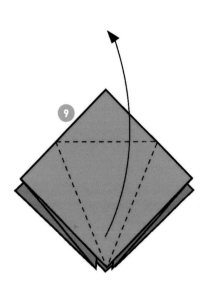

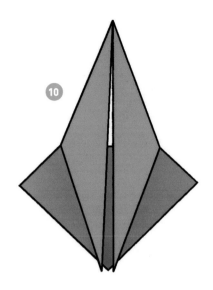

9   Lift the tip like you see in the image.

10   Spread out the tip until you get a long diamond.

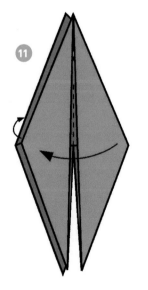

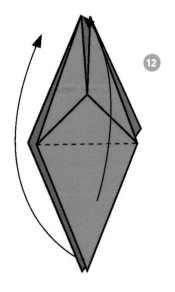

11   Flip the object around 180°.

12   Fold along the line and lift the tips. You've just made a bird base.

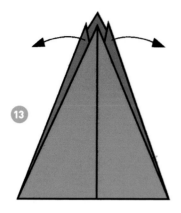

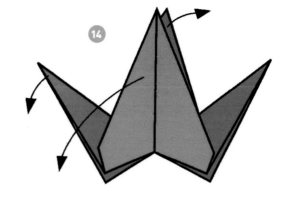

13 Pull the two opposite tips apart like you see in the picture.

14 Pull down the wings and bend one of the tips to make a beak.

PEACOCK

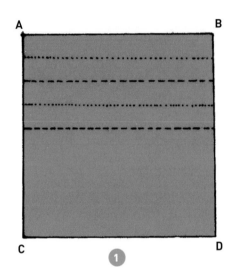

1 Fold the dashed lines forward and the dotted lines backward all along one half of the horizontal axis, making a crease pattern. Next, make an accordion fold by stacking these segments on top of each other.

2 Rotate the figure and fold it forward along the lines.

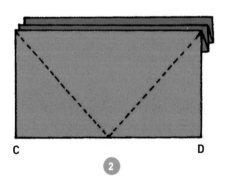

3 Fold forward again along the dotted lines.

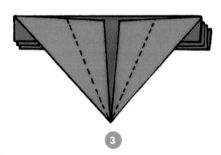

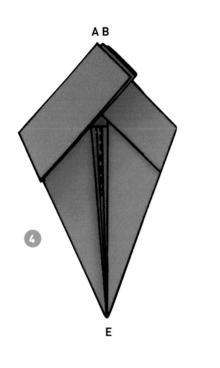

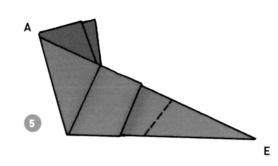

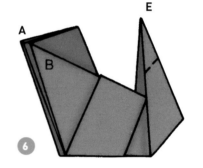

4-5 Now fold the middle line forward. Rotate the figure.

6 With an inside-out fold, bring tip E outward and upward, that is, perpendicular to the base, like in the picture.

7 Fold tip E forward. Now you have the head of the peacock. Open up the tail like a fan.

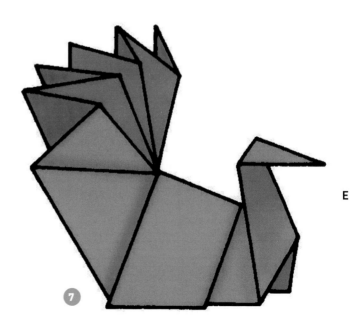

CROW

1-2   Fold along the lines.

3   Fold backwards.

4   Fold the tip and unfold.

5   Fold along the line.

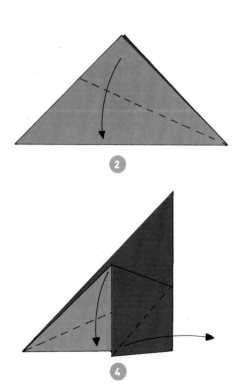

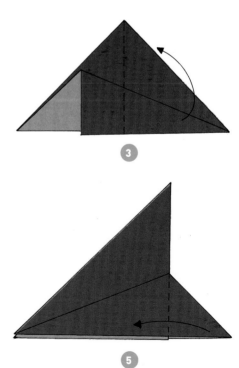

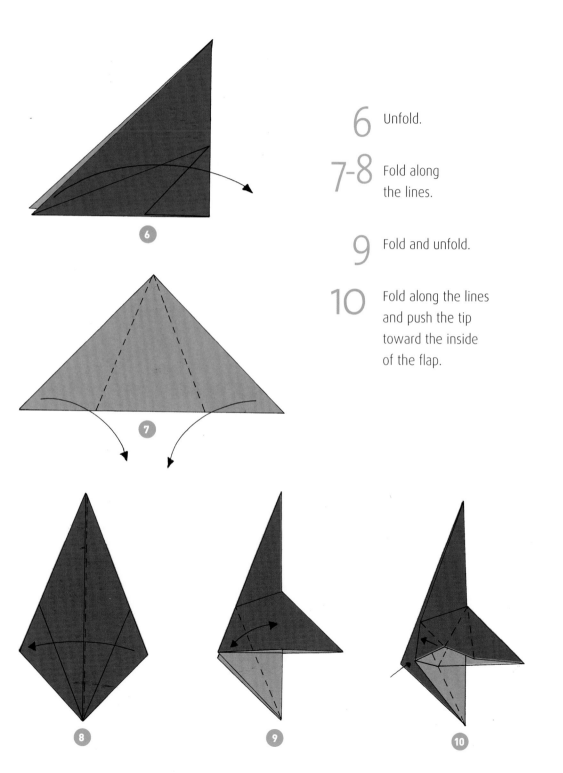

6   Unfold.

7-8   Fold along the lines.

9   Fold and unfold.

10   Fold along the lines and push the tip toward the inside of the flap.

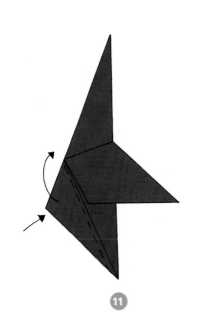
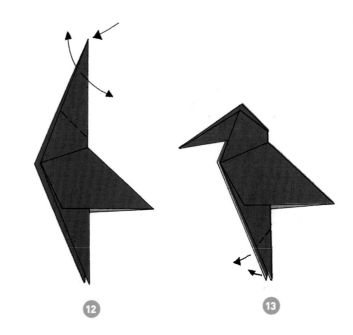

11   Repeat the last step on the other side.

12   Fold the tip in both directions, and then fold it forward to make the head.

13   Fold the bottom tips forward to create the feet.

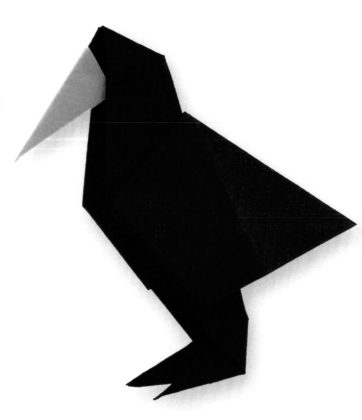

SWAN

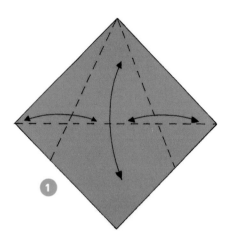

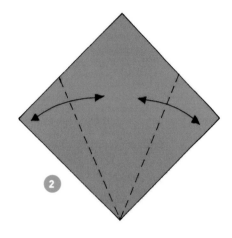

1-2   Fold along the lines and unfold.

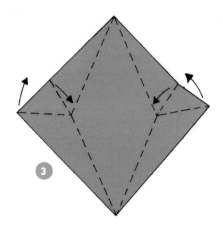

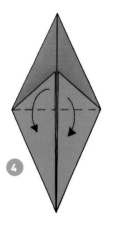

3   Fold and lift the side corners, following the arrows.

4   Once you have an elongated diamond, fold the upper parts of the two middle flaps down.

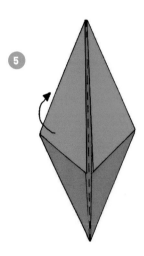

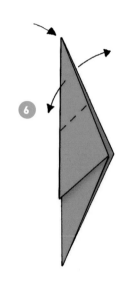

5 Fold the figure in half along the vertical axis.

6-7 Fold the tip forward and in between the fold; rotate the figure.

8 Fold the opposite tip inside the center fold, so it almost touches the previous fold.

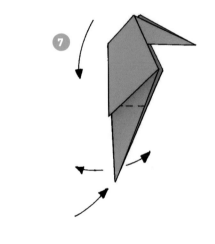

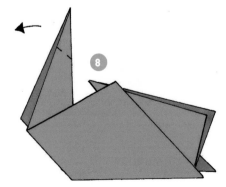

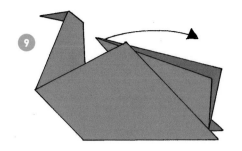

9   Fold the previous fold backward to create a tail.

10   Shape the beak by gently pushing it inside the neck.

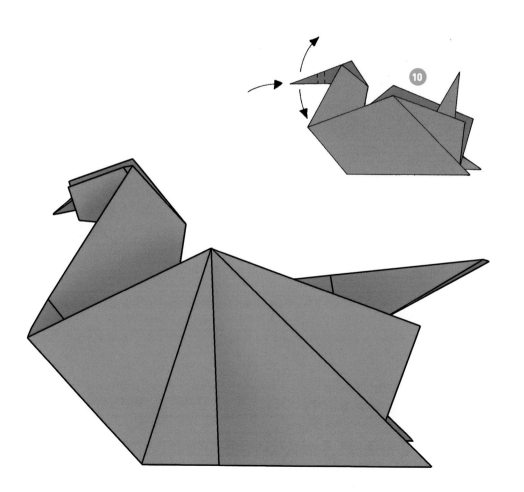

SWALLOW

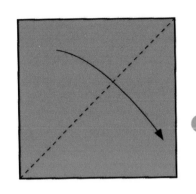

1-3 Fold a square sheet of paper and unfold.

4 Fold inward by bringing the corners together, following the image.

5 Now you have what's called a preliminary base.

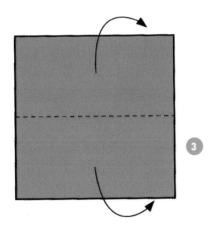

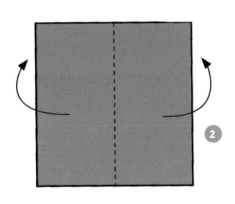

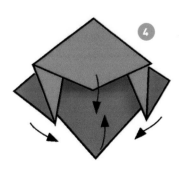

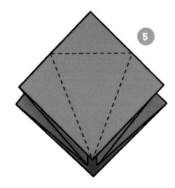

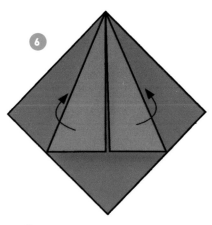

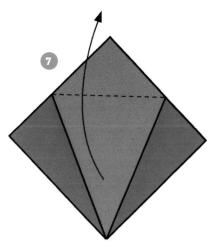

6 Fold the upper part along the lines shown in image 5, slipping the flaps inside.

7 Lift the lower corner up.

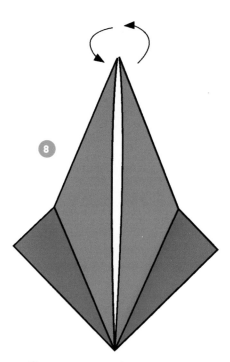

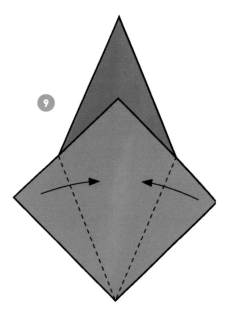

8 Spread it out and you will get an elongated diamond. Rotate the figure.

9 Repeat the last step on the other side.

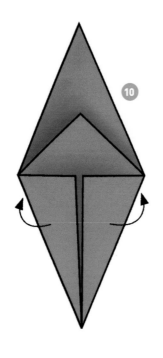

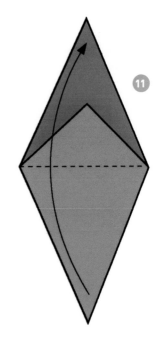

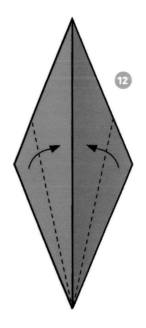

10   Now unfold the folded flaps.

11   Lift the lower point to match the other side.

12   Fold inward along the lines.

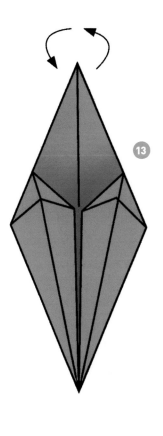

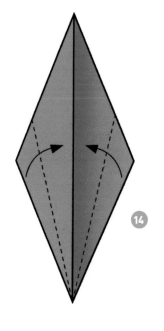

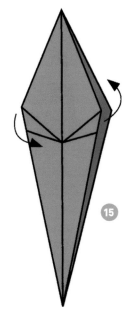

13 Turn the figure over.

14 Fold along the lines, like in the image.

15 Fold the opposite flaps as if they were pages of a book: fold the left flap toward the right, and the right flap toward the left.

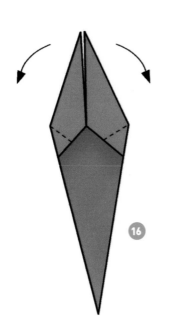

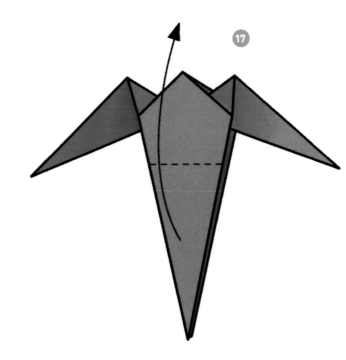

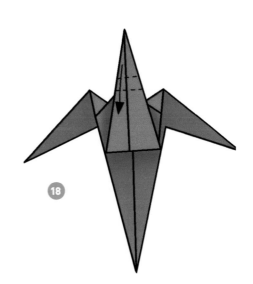

16 Now you'll have a slightly different shape.

17 Fold the upper part along the line and lift the tip.

18 Fold the tip along both lines on the side shown in the image to make the head.

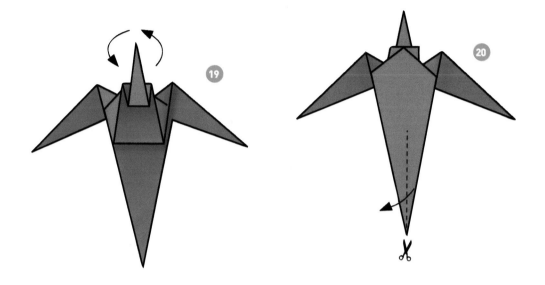

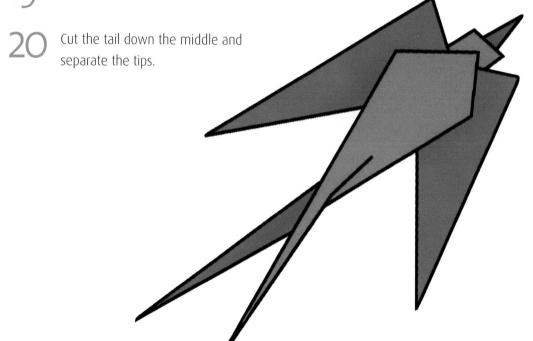

19 Turn it over.

20 Cut the tail down the middle and
separate the tips.

CRANE

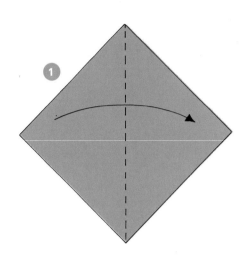

1 Fold a square sheet of paper diagonally.

2 Fold the sheet in half along its vertical axis.

3 Open the first layer.

4 Bring the tips together with squash folds.

5 Turn it over.

6 Bring these tips together as well.

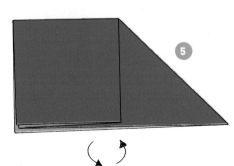

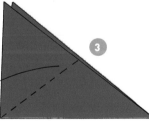

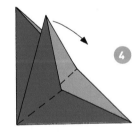

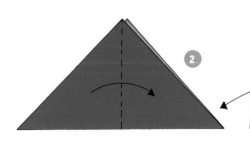

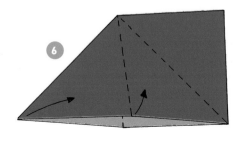

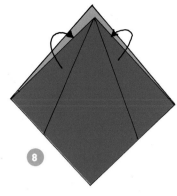

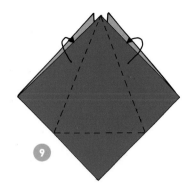

7 Now you have a preliminary base to work with.

8 Fold in both directions and unfold. Fold the two side flaps backward, following the arrows.

9 Repeat the same step on the other side, folding the outer flaps.

10 Fold the tip all the way down, making a squash fold so the paper lays flat.

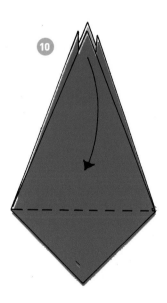

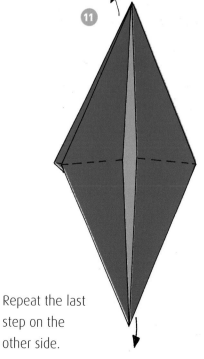

11 Repeat the last step on the other side.

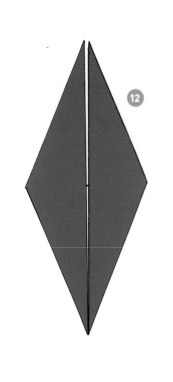

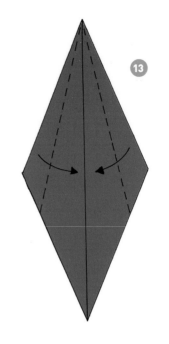

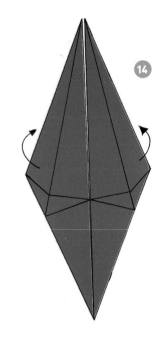

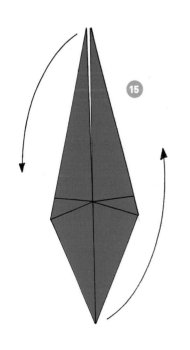

12 Flatten the new object to create your bird base.

13 Fold along the lines.

14 Fold the same way on the other side.

15 Rotate.

16 Fold along the line.

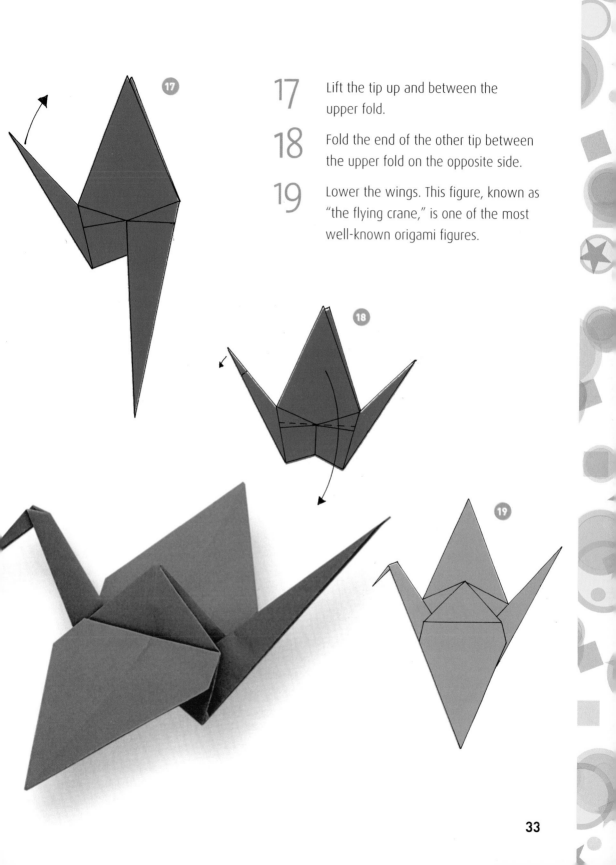

17 Lift the tip up and between the upper fold.

18 Fold the end of the other tip between the upper fold on the opposite side.

19 Lower the wings. This figure, known as "the flying crane," is one of the most well-known origami figures.

TURKEY

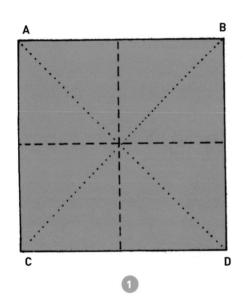

1 Fold backward along the diagonal lines AD and BC two times. Unfold and fold forward along the central lines two times, then unfold.

2 Fold corners B and D over A. Now fold corner A over C.

3 Now fold corners F and G along the lines and unfold. Fold corner E along line 2.

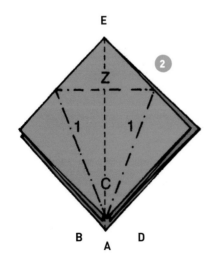

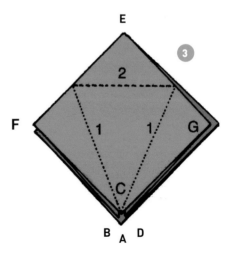

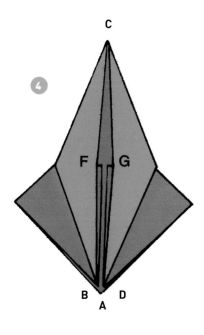

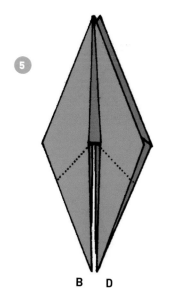

4 Now fold corner C along line 2. At the same time, press F and G along the central line.

5 Rotate the figure and repeat the same steps on the opposite side.

6 Now fold tips B and D inward. Fold tip C forward.

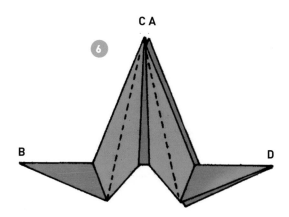

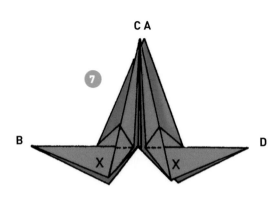

7 Bring the two X corners up along the dotted line.

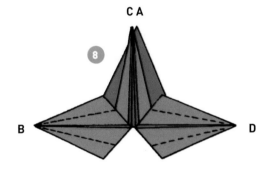

8 Fold tips B and D foward and fold tip A downward.

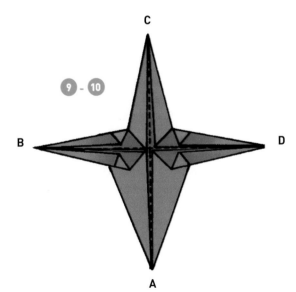

9 Fold tips B and D downward along the fold you have already made. Fold forward along the central line. Rotate the figure.

10 Bring tip C and fold outward. To make the turkey's legs, take tips B and D and fold inward and outward.

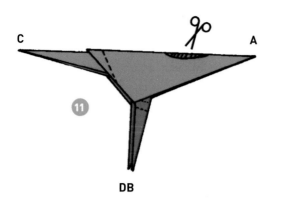

C   A

DB

11   Cut the marked area.

12   Take tip C and fold inward and outward. Now you'll have the head and beak of your turkey.

13   Fold tip A inward.

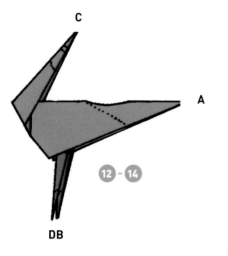

C

A

12 - 14

DB

14   Make the legs by folding tips B and D outward.

15   Fold a sheet of paper like an accordion. Insert one end into the turkey and open it out like a fan.

SPARROW

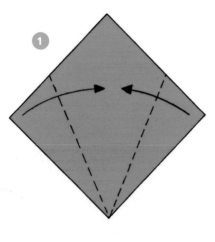

1 Fold along the lines.

2 Fold the flap backward.

3 Fold and lift the right center corner.

4 Bring down the tip and spread it flat.

5 Repeat the last step on the other side.

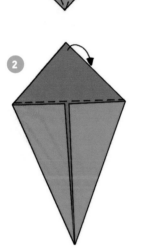

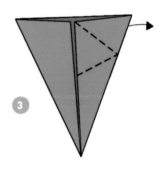

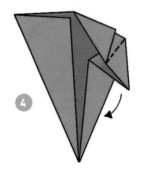

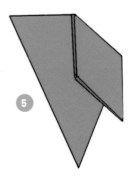

6 Fold both tips like you see
   in the picture.

7 Fold along the line.

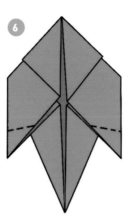

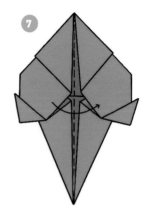

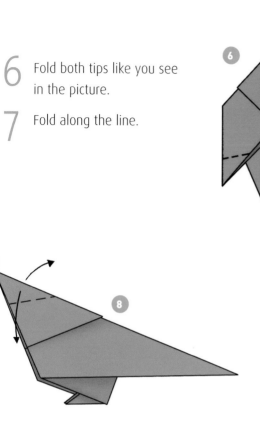

8 Fold down and bring the tip
   inside the flap.

9 Fold the tip of the tail along
   the lines in both directions
   and push it inward.

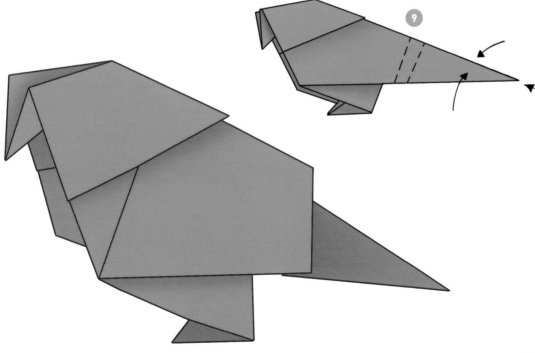

WILD DUCK

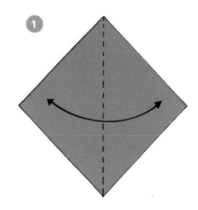

1-2 Fold along the lines and unfold.

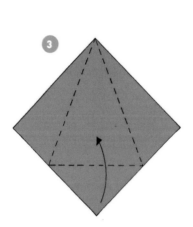

3-4 Fold along the lines.

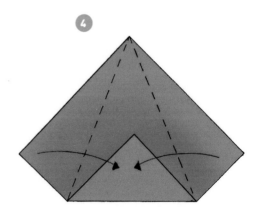

5-6 Lift the flaps and fold them, creating a 180° angle.

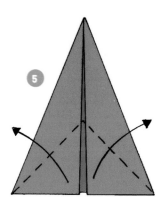

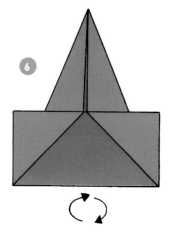

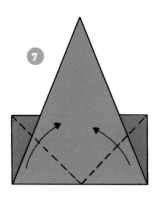

7 Fold along the lines.

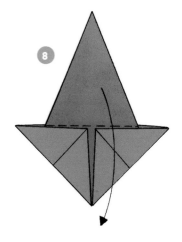

8 Bring the tip down.

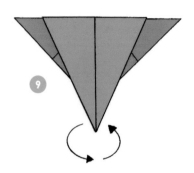

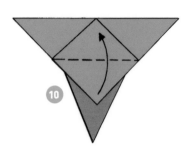

9   Turn it over.

10   Lift the flap and fold it along the line.

11   Fold in half and push the upper part inside.

12   Rotate 180°.

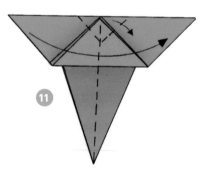

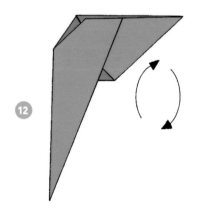

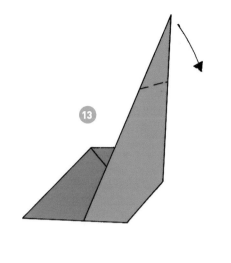

13 Fold the tip in both directions and push it outward.

14 Fold along the lines in both directions and push the tip backward.

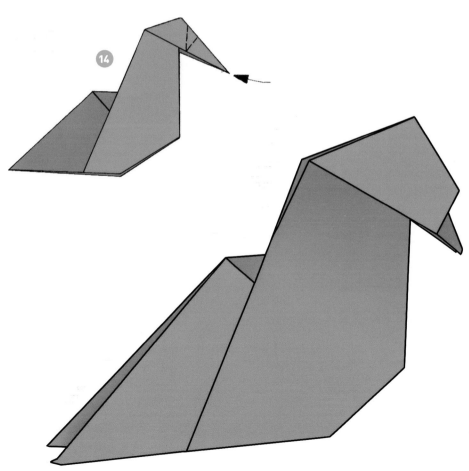

PENGUIN

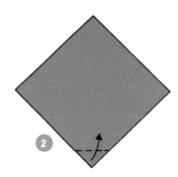

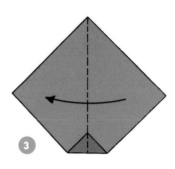

1 Fold a square sheet of paper along the diagonal line and unfold.

2-4 Fold along the lines.

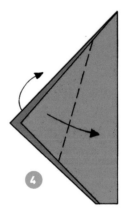

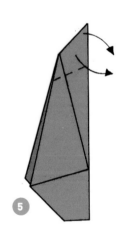

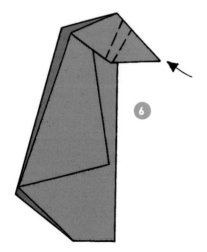

5-6 Fold along the marked line and bring the tip forward. Bend and shape the beak.

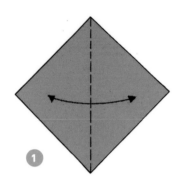

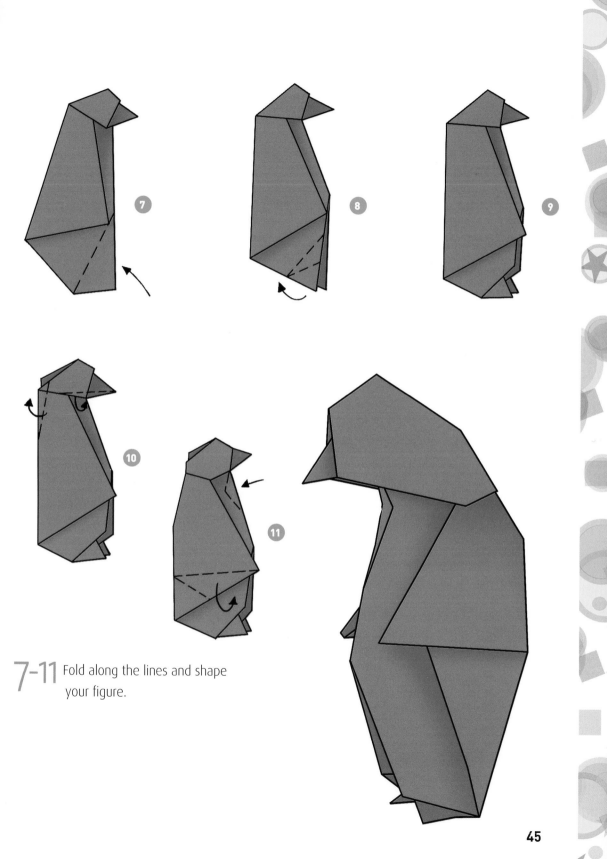

$7\text{-}11$ Fold along the lines and shape your figure.

GLOSSARY

accordion fold A folding technique done by creating a series of parallel creases and folding the paper over itself, mimicking the folds of an accordion.

bird base A variation of a preliminary base used for many figures. Fold the outer points of the preliminary base inward along the vertical axis, and, using this crease pattern, flip the upper layers on each side to the uppermost vertical point.

crease pattern Patterns made from folding and unfolding the paper, often used as guides for the folding process.

horizontal axis Any line running width-wise along the paper.

preliminary base One of the primary bases of origami, made by folding a square paper into quarters and then squash folding two flaps to make a double-layered diamond.

squash fold Any fold done by lifting a flap perpendicular to the paper surface, opening the flap, and spreading the flap flat to create a new surface.

vertical axis Any line running length-wise along the paper.

FURTHER READING

Books

Friedman, Seth. *Bird Origami.* San Diego, CA: Thunder Bay Press, 2015.

Harbo, Christopher. *Origami Palooza: Dragons, Turtles, Birds, and More!* North Mankato, MN: Cap Stone, 2015.

Miles, Lisa. *Origami Birds and Butterflies.* New York, NY: Gareth Stevens, 2014.

Montroll, John. *Origami Birds.* Mineola, NY: Dover Publications, 2013.

Websites

Origami-Fun

www.origami-fun.com

Offers origami diagrams, tips, and articles for all skill levels.

Origami-Instructions

www.origami-instructions.com/

Contains instructions for many origami projects, including flowers, toys, and stars.

Origami Resource Center

www.origami-resource-center.com

Provides dozens of free tutorials and introductions into fabric folding and kirigami (paper cutting).

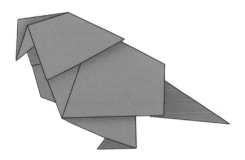

INDEX

A

accordion fold 16, 37

B

beak 7, 10, 15, 23, 37, 44
bird base 14, 32

C

crane **30-33**
crease pattern 16
crow **18-20**

D

diamond 21, 25

F

feet 20

H

head 7, 17, 20, 28, 37
hen **8-11**
horizontal axis 6, 16

L

legs 7, 36, 37

O

owl 4, **6-7**

P

paper 4, 5, 6, 13, 24, 30, 31, 37, 44
peacock **16-17**
penguin 4, **44-45**
preliminary base 24, 31

S

sparrow 4, **38-39**
squash fold 30, 31
stork **12-15**
swallow **24-29**

T

tail 7, 11, 17, 23, 29, 39
turkey **34-37**

V

vertical axis 22, 30, 39

W

wild duck **40-43**